# MOTION TRAILS

## SONGS BY CASPIAN SAWCZAK

# MOTION TRAILS

## SONGS BY CASPIAN SAWCZAK

### EDITED BY LUKE SAWCZAK

*Life Rattle Press* • *Toronto, Canada*

Published in Canada
by
Life Rattle Press
196 Crawford St.
Toronto, Ontario M6J 2V6

*liferattle.ca*



Library and Archives Canada Cataloguing in Publication

Sawczak, Caspian, 1988-, author
Motion trails : songs / by Caspian Sawczak ;
Luke Sawczak.

(New publishers series, ISSN 1713-8981)
Poems.
ISBN 978-1-927023-95-2 (pbk.)

I. Sawczak, Luke, 1991-, editor
II. Title.
III. Series: New publishers series

PS8637.A927M68 2015   C811'.6   C2015-901573-1

Cover design by Aaron Sawczak.
Cover photo by Luke Sawczak.

# A NOTE ON STRUCTURE

This collection is divided into five parts, but the nature of the division is not immediately apparent. They are not, for example, the album on which each song first appeared, the fidelity to which grouping has not been attempted here. Rather, they represent a narrative movement. The songs occupy many different points in terms of tone and subject, but they share elements of style and often (subtly) echo each other verbally and musically. The effect of this is that invisible links emerge from the reading and rereading. What we have tried to do is identify one potential set of links, namely a drama whose acts are suggested by the subtitles and the placement of the songs—partly because we felt a sense of adventure as we did.

If other readings suggest themselves to our readers we are more than content.

# CONTENTS



## CLOSE YET FAR AWAY



## NOTHING TOO PROFOUND

# BANDAGES AND IODINE



# THE WINDS PREVAILING



# MOTION TRAILS

# PREFACE

*LUKE SAWCZAK*

*Here we are, the strong, the weak, and the mild,*
*and our integrity is going fast out of style.*

When I first encountered these lyrics in my older brother Cas's song "The Rest We Know", I was immediately inclined to alter them. Thus it was that in a high school New Testament class I went up and wrote on the whiteboard:

*Here we are, the strong, the weak, and the mild,*
*and we are hoping we will soon be reconciled.*

To my mind, my version had several advantages. For one, it was a full rhyme, not a half-rhyme. For another, the beat landed on "*rec-oncile*", rather than "*out* of style", and only the former is naturally stressed. Besides, the message seemed more straightforward to me, never mind the fact that it was fundamentally different. I didn't know what "the integrity" of each element meant. And if I could have done something equally bold to that first line, which to me suggested a line of coffees, I would have.

My teacher, John Terpstra, read what I'd written while I explained where it'd come from and how my keen editing eye had improved it.

"Actually, I like the original better," he said. "He's saying that the trend of the day is to break down barriers, which is all well and good, but that there are some things that really are distinct. Some things have integrity, a unique identity, and they might lose it if we blend them together without discrimination."

I couldn't argue with that.

I had already begun to enjoy Cas's music, but this was the first time I considered that what my brother sang in his mostly punk rock songs, the ones we at home heard him taking and retaking (though he had at least abandoned screamo), might actually be profound and poetic. His instincts might in fact be more reliable than mine. So I set aside my editorializing and just listened.

Since then I have listened to as much of Cas's back catalogue as I can get—there are a few tracks I don't have copies of. I have listened to it all many times. I listen to it as I drive, work, play, and write, though there are breaks of a few months between great draughts of it. The music has not lost its charm over the years, but the lyrics have gained much more. Every few verses I encounter another such epigrammatic couplet to share with my friends or to dwell on myself.

What is perhaps ironic about this collection, indeed any printed collection of lyrics, in light of the preceding is that its essential project is a reconciliation of music and poetry. Music proper and poetry proper diverged long ago—despite the oft-quoted assertion that poetry is basically musical—excepting the phenomena of opera and song. Caspian's work isn't opera; and song, whether in the folk expression of centuries past or in the explosion of the instantly consumable $0.99 single, has rarely been regarded as a high art worthy of codification.

When Bruce Cockburn came to the Toronto Reference Library last November to speak about his memoir, I stood up during the Q&A at the end and asked a (rambling) question I would reformulate along these lines: Simon and Schuster has just put out a 900-page volume of Bob Dylan's lyrics. Your own songs are considered lyrically strong, something not every songwriter puts before the music, and you said you began by writing poetry in high school. Would you set your own song lyrics down on paper? Can lyrics be literature?

"The song lyrics I write are intended to be heard with music," he answered. "You make compromises with language when you're trying to fit it to music, or fit music to it, and there's some back and forth … If I was writing for the page there would be fewer prepositions and fewer adjectives, and the rhythm would be different. I don't think of my own song lyrics as poetry exactly. They're poetic, I hope. But I've never liked the idea of putting out a book of them to be encountered away from the music."

The exceptions might include his spoken word songs, he said, and almost anything by Leonard Cohen, but "In general, you can sing, 'Row, row, row your boat', but reading it sucks."

So the challenge of converting something written for music into something I can only present to you here in silence is a real one. But the problem is more nuanced than that. If there are exceptions due either to special talent or to having ignored musical limitations, how do you identify and isolate them? What if you might have some on your hands? After all, we are not dealing with "Row, row, row your boat". Rather:

*If all else fails*
*say it's all in the moment*
*a passionate sort of thing*
*"spirit in motion".*

("Motion Trails")

The particulars of the challenge arose in the editing (which, although the bulk was done by myself, also underwent Cas's revision and has his approval). What became immediately apparent was that it was far from entirely a matter of undoing the compromises Cockburn speaks of. That is, a poem does not emerge from the mere deleting of prepositions and adjectives and rhythmic props. Nor, as I found after my first pass, did beginning every line with a lowercase letter make a poem, nor disguising the most obvious rhymes with line breaks, nor eliminating each nonverbal "oh" and "yeah" or reinserting the first syllable of each "because". Of course, such changes do affect the reading and have contributed in varying measures to the final form of the poems. But in the end they are superficial and often did not ring true.

Even when confronting only the bare lyrics, only what you have transcribed, you must wrestle with the ghost of the absent. What music contributes to the meaning of a song cannot be overstated. Should you repeat a chorus in the text? The first instinct is no: a poet rarely needs to repeat the same block of lines unless for effect, because the quality of poetry is the unique utterance. But if you do not repeat a chorus you sometimes end up with two verses in a row in which the second has clearly responded to something, and the invisibility of that something is more frustrating than suggestive. Sometimes, it feels quite unfairly, an instrumental bridge can be the developing force in the narrative of a song: in the hearing something happens that allows you to come to the end of the song a different listener, but the means of saying it is irreproducible in writing.

I felt like giving up, but when I told this to Cas he suggested that rather than try to make the material exactly conformable to poetry, and end up with something too transparently altered, I could let the original stand in places and change it in others. If this or that must be repeated, let it be. It might not be strictly poetry, but better to keep it than to remove the support of another part of the structure. Fair enough, I thought; it was in this form I heard the work in the first place and believed it could stand up on the page. If it had really had as far to go as I was trying to push it, I might not have had that reaction. Hence what you will read is mostly the product of a light touch, without apology for lines that suggest a musical origin if it was the best option.

And anyhow there is something to be said for this middle road; lyrics are not merely words at the mercy of music, but an interplay between the two, and some aspect of this interesting exchange can indeed be captured in a book. I can't help but recall a particular (early) chorus of Dylan's:

> *You say you're looking for someone*
> *who will promise never to part,*
> *someone to close his eyes for you,*
> *someone to close his heart,*
> *someone who will die for you and more—*
> *but it ain't me, babe,*
> *no, no, no, it ain't me, babe,*
> *it ain't me you're looking for, babe.*
>
> ("It Ain't Me, Babe", 1964)

Musically as well as on the page "more" is set up to rhyme perfectly with "for", and each chorus has the same rhyme. The musical phrase also returns satisfyingly to the root on "for". The final "babe" comes in halfway through the last bar and is invariably surprising.

When I first heard this I asked Cas, "Why would he ruin it? It's perfect without that last 'babe'!"

"It took me a long time to understand why he did that, too, but now I realize he couldn't have done it any other way," he replied.

This was another lesson for me, a subtle shift out of my assumptions, like the one I'd gotten from John Terpstra. The exact appeal of the final "babe" is hard to identify. True, the other two "babe"s also interrupt their bars halfway through. But this observation does not account for the fact that the last "babe" is more interesting than the first two. My suspicion is that the words and the music anticipate and try to surprise each other. The final "babe" fills the verbal pattern and hence sounds inevitable, but to do so it must stand outside the musical mould and hence sounds misplaced (like, a friend points out, the lover's affection). Likewise, the lines both rhyme and do not: taking the musically significant elements they rhyme in a straightforward way, but counting the entire utterance we have instead a feminine last rhyme. Taking the whole picture, the lyrics and music together, such paradoxes are possible. And the magic is that each part taken on its own has the power of suggesting the missing element.

Such a discussion might seem hopelessly unpoetic, glorifying nothing, like hanging a child's stick figures in a gallery. After all, who would bother to argue about this or that instance of a throwaway word like "babe"? But this is only an analysis of a simple folk piece and, to my mind at least, yields a whiff of evidence for the claim that song can be high art, childlike lyrics and all. How much more so when it comes to Cohen's or Cockburn's or Caspian's songs, in which the words are carefully chosen and can stand quite formidably on their own.

The only section of this book whose title is taken from a song we eventually rejected is "Nothing Too Profound". Besides being a characteristically modest comment by the author on his own in fact significant feelings, it also represents the perspective a careless reader might be tempted to take on the whole work. Indeed these are songs; they cannot and should not be disguised as pure poetry. Indeed they do not exist the same way in a musical vacuum as they do in a pair of earbuds. But they still carry with them the marks of their original form, marks that contribute to their character; and they are no less than art for it.

*Georgetown*
*April 2015*

# CLOSE
# YET
# FAR AWAY

## TAKE IT IN STRIDE

Well, I'd like a holiday,
but my body's in the way.
Sometimes I live in fiction;
sometimes I love the addiction.

Well, I'm bored, smoking on the porch.
I don't know what I'm here for.
Lock the windows,
lock the doors.

Imaginary friends I've made,
well, they help to animate
still life on frozen frames.
It's my hero and my bane.

Oh no—a year ago
I wasn't moving quite so slow.

And I will not be afraid
to live with the choices I have made.

Once in a while I cannot breathe
and I'd rather die than take the heat.
Seems life is drifting out of reach.

And every night
the world ends in my dreams.

The more I speak my mind,
the more I fall behind.
Sometimes I talk on paper.
Sometimes I find it safer.

It's all right, I'll take it in stride.
No need to apologize.
Cross your fingers,
cross your eyes.

And I will not be afraid
to live with the choices I have made.

Sometimes what's real I cannot tell.
The fear of failure—I know it well.
You've got to break out of your shell.
Before you walk through Heaven
you gotta run through Hell.

Stand back in battle season;
look around and call it even.

Well, I tried a holiday.
Looks like I'm here to stay...

So I'll find another way.

## CANADA GEESE SONG

The summer's holding the fall at bay.
It's time to trade my old feathers away.
I need a brand new plane,
there's little time to spare.
The river stops in its tracks,
we take to the air.

It's far too late for the winter.
She's our playmate and splinter,

death radiating in her.

The sages are feeling the season die.
The children don't understand
but they don't ask why.
The admiral is showing
the bars of his years;
ready for the burn,
he has no fear.

When the season
is much longer
than you bargained for,
it's a natural reaction
to be bored.

Our captain knows
the way to go
to find our home.
How high we get
like smoother jets
we're black sails
in the sunset.

Danger awaits
wherever we fly.
A farmer's field,
a good day to die.
Hunters
hunting with gunpowder,
getting closer,
getting louder.

And in the clouds
your vision is blown.
You cease to exist,
you're flying
on your own.

But we are the free
and very much awake.
We will go
wherever it takes us.

When the season's ending
so unfair
and you're not prepared,
it's a natural reaction
to be scared.

Our captain knows
the way to go
to find our home.
How high we get
like smoother jets
we're black sails
in the sunset.

## SLEEPWALK TO REASON

Another day,
another chance for me to fail you.
Ran away from all those days I knew you.
So fleeting,
my heart chases the world.

I see no way out.

Find a hold,
only to slip from it.
It's kinda cold;
only your flame can overcome it.
Still sleeping,
on my own I'm good as dead.

On my own...

The dawn of the night, sleepwalking
sixty times to a minute
"I think you might this time—"

Would you let me finish?
All meaning
gone from this ritual.

Last resort:
wipe the tears.
Just like a holiday:
insincere,
always short, always a lie.

There's too much me, not enough time—
too much me, not enough time for you.

I stop at six for a goodbye
and then I call this a highlight.

I waste life like it was mine
and then I call this a highlight.

Yeah, you'd think it was mine,
all my time.

## *NOLA*

There's a hurricane
missed me by a mile.

Katrina and her floods
came screaming down
on the jazz capital of the lovely South.

The place was already below sea level
so you can imagine how it looked
and just how little time it took
to fold them like a deck of playing cards.

And it blows my mind away
how cavalier
we all are over here.

Lady New Orleans
will never be the same.

It's ironic in a dry and raw way:
the enforcers of the law, it seems,
are now breaking it
just like human beings.

It looks like we're just animals
when things get desperate
(should have guessed it).

And the vast majority
of the people trapped in the city
just happened to be
not white,
not wealthy,
not lucky.

It scares me just how
close
yet far away
we are from yesterday.

In the ruin
that once was New Orleans,
the old city full of music, lights, and dreams,
I can see the old men drinking and playing
    cards,
just like my boss said.

*PLAYING IT SAFE*


Are we for real,
or are we just
playing it safe?

You know it's just
a matter of the time it takes
to make a mess of the situation,
no course,
no destination.

And I feel brave,
but I feel braver
when you tell me
you never need a reason.
So for what are you holding out?

Rain's really coming down
somewhere,
making or breaking love.

And each and every mirror
that you break apart:
seven more years.
Each piece
shows a part of you

that you thought I forgot.
But every scene is missing.
I forget what we were wishing for.

And I feel brave,
but I feel braver
when you tell me
you never need a reason.
So for what are you holding out?

Watch it come
crashing down tonight,
somewhere,
making or breaking love.

*TEMPORARY*

Sunny day, soul rotation
the Tragic and Sublime
Mixing up the information
It gets me every time

Where are my senses?
(I can't feel myself)
Where are my defences?
(I don't need your help)

'cause it's all temporary
(Dog-paddle out of the shallow end)
Never dead and buried
is what just might rise again

Stock up on cloak-and-dagger
paraphernalia
and one of these days we will go
to Australia

The skies are talking to me
(The clouds can read my mind)
I never knew they knew me
(You never know what you'll find)

Never dead and buried
is what just might...

And I will fight this battle
even if the odds are slim to none
because knowing all the answers
never was much fun

Blame the engineering
kill the lights one by one
when everything's disappearing
the smoother it will run

And you know these kinds of moments
are few and far between
Have you lost track of the stolen,
the borrowed, and the clean?

It's all temporary
(Dog-paddle out of the shallow end)
Never dead and buried
is what just might rise again
It's all temporary
In the morning I'll pretend
we're in Montréal again

# NOTHING TOO PROFOUND

## SOME CARELESS NOTE

Waves that rise and fall but never change at
    all
What broke? I heard some careless note
tossed on a hook like a worm
like a coat

This spinning rock we're living on?
Backwards all along.

That is how
we all get paid
That is why
the starlight left
and the neon stayed.

Well, I don't want to remember it, but I had a
    nightmare
We were up against the numbers
and the numbers don't fight fair
Someone yelled "We're under attack!"
Trafalgar Road was a river of black

"We don't get rainbows in our sky
the taxes are too high"

Could've sworn the gremlins died
but now there's more
(how did they survive? must have multiplied)

The Ides of March and wounded hearts
don't get me started stop playing the part
one was trampled to death at a sale at
    Walmart
(coffin was a shopping cart)
They got rid of Marilyn Monroe
'cause she knew too much—royal trust and
    such

You're on your own
    (are you stoned?)

That UFO won't leave you alone
That bird has flown

## COBWEBS IN YOUR ATTIC

long way there
long way back
I'm not sure
I've lost track

chains of time
chains of emotion
either way
our tongues are frozen

and when it's time to go
you suffer one embrace
you know I missed you so
I think we need the space

we're giving up the chase

and before your life goes on
I know I'm already gone

on rooftops in stormy weather
no better place to be together
give me your burdens to carry
I'd rather fall with you
than fly solitary

and when we do
we'll play it out like our hearts are
see-through

**WORDS THAT I PRAY (LOSING SLEEP)**

Unless
I find you anytime soon,
    I'll make believe I'm quite immune.

All this time we spend
underneath the ever-faithful moon...
    don't you ever feel marooned?

Unless
you've got better things to do...
    'cause I wouldn't want to make you stay
    longer than you meant to.

Could you flutter down
from beyond the blue?
    Don't you ever feel marooned?

My life's a desert,
you're a perfect mirage...

I could never be
farther from pure,
and where I'll end up
I'm not entirely sure.
I am the sickness

and you're probably the cure.

Is any one of us completely secure?

Unless
you've got better people to see...
    'cause I wouldn't want to make you lose
    sleep over me.

Could you carry me
beyond the blue?
    Don't you ever feel marooned
      in this crowded room?

My life's a sketch,
you're a quaint collage...

I could never be
farther from pure,
and where I'll end up
I'm not entirely sure.
I am the sickness
and you're probably the cure.

When you are near
I feel completely secure.

*FIREFLIES*


Escape is narrow
when the trap is wide.
Look for the arrow
and follow it outside.
Am I getting closer
or straying from the truth?
I need somebody
or the great blue sky
to fall into.

There will be justice and freedom,
rest assured,
from all your shadows
and the voices that you've heard.
Come all ye faithful,
bring the light of day!
Just you and I and the fireflies...
baby, would you stay?

I caught your stare.
You found me there
with your dark, stormy eyes
and your angel's hair.

Do you wonder—

I'm scared to ask—
do you ever wonder
if we could be something
that could last?

You at the doorstep,
me waiting on the road:
Valentine's Day,
taking care not to drop your present in the
    snow.
Why did I come here
if you're just going to go?
Yeah, you're killing me,
but it's you that's keeping me alive,
you know?

We lay in darkness.
I knew it wasn't fate,
hoping we could change that
if there ever was a way.
'cause I am a dreamer,
and baby, so are you.
But if you walk away from me
I know
there's nothing
I can do.

I caught your stare.
You found me there
with your dark, stormy eyes
and your angel's hair.

Do you wonder—
I'm scared to ask—
do you ever wonder
if we could be something?

Sometimes I wish
I never turned around.
I could have kept on walking
and forgot about the sound
of your voice and laughter,
the song I thought
would drown out
all the darkness in my world...
In you a brighter world I found.

## THE REST WE KNOW

Somebody got you to rock
and they showed you the way.
Somebody got you to talk
and gave you things to say.

Somebody got you to own up to
all of your good deeds
and your wicked seeds.
Somebody got you to call up the cops
on the quack doctor
calling for cough drops.

The rest we know.

Somebody got you to shop
and to cut off the tags.
Somebody got you to drop them
in the garbage bags.

Somebody got you to fool around
with the building blocks
and the grandfather clocks.
Somebody got you to play the charade
for the cold cash
and the true trash.

The rest we know.

So here we are, the strong,
the weak, and the mild,
and our integrity
is going fast out of style.

But there is nothing we could not create
or could not remove
if we wanted to.
It's too easy,
but too hard to stop,
just right now anyhow.

The rest we know.

*DÉJÀ VU*

Window, show to me
what's wrong with January
'cause in my memory
there's something about the weather
that felt a little better.

What a sticky scenario.
We never really stopped
'cause we thought it wouldn't show.
When will we get enough
of reaping what we sow?
We broke the heart of Mother
and there is no other.

Soon enough we'll pay the price,
stand before the saints of paradise,
and no excuse will quite suffice
'cause we broke the heart of Mother.

When I feel I'm on the brink,
I find solace in a whisky drink
and on occasion I will stop to think,
"No, pull yourself together.
It's fucking now or never."

I think the hippies understood,
and I'm starting to think I should
fake my death and live
in a shack in the woods,
and get to know Mother,
'cause there is no other.

The earth, the sky, the water, and the trees...
it's really all we need,
and all of this was here before us.
I think I'm hearing voices
on the breeze,
 saying,

"Life is granted
If you demand it

Not one stone
will be left standing."

# BANDAGES & IODINE

# FIRE OR A FALSE ALARM

Growing up, never out of line,
waiting for the prince
she was hoping she'd find—
true love taking its sweet time.

She's a lamb, somewhat shy.
She's got a sacred place
in which to fantasize.
She is grace
    and she is charm,
she is dangerous and armed,
but she can't tell true love
from a false alarm.

Where there's smoke
there's fire or a false alarm.

Couldn't tell her to her face:
the love was never even there in the first
    place.
And now her dreams all go to waste;
she never even got a taste.

Please send oxygen,
'cause whatever I am breathing

is affecting my judgement.
But I suppose if it don't show
it's just a surefire way to forget...

Left to your own devices
alone,
with a will to finally conquer
the fear of the unknown.

But burning out, your vision's a haze,
and only deeper, darker questions
the answer will raise.

Simple dreams of simple romance—
she said "I believe in magic,
you've gotta give it a chance."

## MERMAID


in this life there is many a wind
some to kindle and some to rescind
some to abandon and some to embrace
each gale begins to prove
just how much you can take

and it's slowing the Mermaid down

## *MOLLY*

Molly
She always wanted to see the sea
She wept while the world sang harmfully
On the way, all the way,
    she sang to me.

Molly
She knew the secrets behind the signs
She knew the source of this pain of mine
On the way
    she whispered to me:

"Storm's coming. Find a hero, take hold.
It won't save your life—
    it'll save your soul."

Sunday,
I scored a boat just for Molly and me
We set out to float on the blue-green sea
We watched the waves,
and the waves
    watched Molly and me.

Dusk
brought the wind that would shake my world
Dusk raised up the water
    and said, "I'll take your girl."
Dusk,
a nightmare to be,

    tortured me
    on the tortured sea
    That's where I lost my world.

When the storm came I saw no heroes,
but Molly wasn't cold.
It didn't save her life—
    it saved her soul.

And when the wind was blowing,
Molly looked so free,
and I saw her shut her eyes so celestially.
The ocean air, the girl, an epiphany:

    Molly's hero wasn't me.

REACH


God knows how I got so lucky
or if I ever will again
there are times I want to reach you
times I want to speak to you again

I'm a little bit grey and shaded
out of touch
    dissociated
never would occur to me
stars matching her and me
all of us breathing
    set fire to the melody

all I know is it's just a little strange
if you don't feel nothin at all
you gotta get out
gotta get yourself somewhere else
it's a ride
or a spot in the harbour

So get yourself free
I'm here if you need me

daydreams about time machines
and going back

'cause I remember
dancing on the lawn
till the day was all gone
I promise you I'll
give you that same smile

all I know is it's just a little lame
if you don't feel nothin at all
you gotta get out
gotta get yourself somewhere else
and I don't mean the place
on the postcard, baby

get yourself free
I'm here if you need me

I'm a little bit grey and shaded
out of touch
    dissociated
you're something so new to me
speaking green and blue to me
two of us breathing
    set fire to the melody

## STORM THE CASTLE

The chance to believe it
either you take it or you leave it
The chance to be naked
why wouldn't you take it?

You could play it safe;
the coffee shops are open.
But your trusty satellite keeps you hoping
that there's something better outside.
Greener grass
kept alive by the pesticide.

You can't go to sleep without a nightlight.

The chance to be open-eyed
why wouldn't that be worth your broken
   pride?
The chance to receive it
either you take it or you leave it

You could play it safe;
the corner stores are open.
But the noise from the highway keeps you
   hoping
that there's something better outside.

Storm the castle
with your bandages and iodine.

After all, it's just another bright light.

The chance to receive it
either you take it or you leave it
The chance to be real
and to really feel
with nothing to conceal

You and me
in and out of independence
finally
found a way around our innocence.
I thought I must be dreaming a whirlwind of
     wonder
two parts winter love and one part good
     summer.

You went back to college
and we moved closer in the fall.
From the Tree of Knowledge
we took another trip to Montréal.
One night on the road we almost died
because the rain was freezing.
That's how it started: my heart
was looking for a reason.

Enough to uncover
laughers loving in colour
from one world to another

You were a painter,
my world became a canvas for your brush.

I was a minstrel,
I serenaded you from dawn till dusk.

Lying in your bed
I heard my Shepherd calling to me,
staring at the ceiling of the Sistine Chapel
falling through me.

And the temple was broken
I lived a year in that moment
with the chariot wheels rolling

I could not stay
living in that way.

I want to sing the sound
of the lost and found.

So every time
I hear your voice or read your words
it brings to mind those feelings...
they all rush by in a blur.

But saying yes to one thing
might mean saying no to another.

And all that I can do
is wish you a good summer.

# THE WINDS PREVAILING

## TORN AND TOSSED


Don't you rush now. The season is new,
but the red of her lips is now closer to blue.

With the veil of summertime lifted
we can see just how far we've drifted.

In just a few weeks, or even days,
all that's green is getting closer to grey.

With the veil of summertime torn and tossed
we can see just how much we've lost.

All the trees
in their nakedness
seem to be out of place in this
climate so misleading,
all the secrets we're keeping.
Winter says she's leaving,
but she'll come back
when we're sleeping.

I once had a vivid vision.
The cold came but the frost was hidden.
The cold came
but the frost was hidden,

forever our shame
because we never listened.

Leaders and pathfinders
and the read-between-the-liners...
The keepers aren't the finders
and this is just a reminder.

## MEET ME WHERE I AM

1

This love is a vehicle
   and sometimes
   feels like a race.
And all the mirrors now
   forecast a change of pace.
Those trips and cozy hotel rooms—
   that's pressure to engage.

So meet me where I am,
   wherever that might be.
Swimming through dry land
   is how it feels to me.
On the Ferris wheel squeezing my hand,
   you never looked so sweet before, so

   meet me where I am.

2

I've been looking for you,
I've been talking to the air.
I've been rocking back and forth
   on that silver chair.

I've been waging wars against myself,
    but I know you're there.

So meet me where I am,
    wherever that might be.
I'm tired of this island,
    I'm heading out to sea.
I remember some faraway shoreline
    where Someone said to me,

    "Meet Me where I Am."

So meet me where I am,
    wherever that might be.
Show me who I am,
    'cause you know better than me.
If I give you all I am,
    will you set me free and more?

    Meet me where I am.

## YOU NEVER STOP LOVING

That snowy night you saved my life
the car spun out and hit the curbside
Figured out you saved me for the next life
Me, I'm not a holy man
The powers I don't understand
I'm just trying to find you in my new life

And you
you came running

In retrospect, I get the sense
all my life you've been there waiting
for me to let you near the light switch
You've been busy fighting for me
making room for me on the second storey
You were pouring out your heart, I said yes

And I'm in
over my head

But you never stop loving, Jesus
Nothing ever stops your love

When I asked forgiveness for my failure
you said, "Son, I don't even remember."

You not only medicate but cure my sickness
It doesn't matter if I'm rich or poor
everything I have is yours
God, help me lay it down at your feet

'cause you
you came kneeling,
you came washing.

Now I need healing,
so I come kneeling.

*SIMPLE LIVING*

I work at a museum
with treasures of the past,
surrounded by a mountain range
and a forest built to last.
It makes me want to build something
with my own two hands—
or just build somebody up...

I was made for simple living.

Never short of inspiration
stumbling after you.
I saw you feed five thousand people—
so what should I do?
Should I knock on every door
to feed five thousand more,
or be a brother to a few?

I want to love like you love.

Every day I fill my time
with stories good and bad.
I don't want to miss the chance to give time
    to you
'cause you're the only chance I have.

So when I see so many open doors,
which ones should I ignore
and which one gets me to you?

I was made for simple living.

I said I wish that I was better
and you asked me what I mean.
I said I wish I was a loving person,
bursting at the seams,
and your answer was a simple one,
since simple's what I need:

So why don't you just love?

## JUST WHAT I LOOK FOR IN AN EXIT

we are comfortable
we are restless
we are capable
of so much more than this

we are impractical
we are animals
something tangible
keeps us here

something unimaginable
something to fear

you tossed the key to every door
without a second more
hesitation
in love with your hallucinations
you said you want to quit
I've had about enough of it

and this is just what I look for
in an exit

we are impractical
are we animals?

something tangible
keeps us going

something unimaginable
something overflowing

some of us get by sailing
driven by the winds prevailing
some of us are a different kind

I just can't quit
and you know where to find me

# MOTION
# TRAILS

## SAND AND SALTWATER

Pictures in your head
are your defence
and ammunition
and on the path ahead
you will come to meet yourself
beyond all recognition

And now the gods that you invent
you must consult
before each decision
with malicious intent
shameless assault
with your permission
with no inhibitions

And the shoreline
is so very vague
on account of your blinded eyes
on account of the plague
In the woods on the mainland
surely grows the cure
but the shoreline
is so obscure

Bring a new face
bring your best ambitions
bring me to a new place
on one condition:
I can leave
once this ship runs aground
I'd love to get home in one piece
safe and sound

Wasted time
is just another consequence
of dreaming up things like this
You never find a way out

If all else fails
say it's all in the moment
a passionate sort of thing
"spirit in motion".

And you always find a way out

I try to change my mind
I know it's only right
another hole in time
I know it's only

Life.

I think of all the chances I have blown
see her drinking coffee all alone.
I'd like to join her (I really should)
if I were a braver man
I would.

Helplessly watch the wind
carry the ashes over the edge
as if it needs to be somewhere fast
I wish I had a wind like that.

Wish I could roll those dice
and never once think twice
I am not myself
but this is just what it looks like
to everybody else.

It was a whole new dark
it was a halfway mark
I'll never live it down
oh no, it's just another thing
to fucking follow me around.

we used to shine
we used to glow
but we have lost it long ago

and when there's no one around
to share the blame
part of me says it's a shame

we used to shine
we used to glow

could we again?
we'll never know

we killed the fun
in record time

out of sight,
out of mind

Am I out of line?...



I want to be moved.

*GARDEN'S ON FIRE*


Three tears say she gave up the race
Violet carnations all over the place

The sheets on her bed purest white
She wishes she was the same inside

Meant to be
We're all out of sincerity

and all she deserves
is every touch of light

The window in her room
lets her whisper to the moon

and pretend it'll all be over soon

Now the garden's on fire

The rain pours down
Flames get higher

Is anybody
a single banner of charity?

All she deserves
An oasis in the night

*PASSERBY*


I am only a passerby
but I can't help but notice
all about you there's something bright
and I want you to know this:

that everything you do
leaves me nothing less
than enchanted and sleepless
scented and speechless

and all I ask is
could I pass by you again?

I am kind of a drifter
not sure where I belong
but these days I break down quicker
so I'll try not to be long

the secrets in your eyes
keep me motionless
and rescue me from the mess
you're a miracle, I guess

and all I ask is
could I drift by you again?

## BATMAN

I've known you since last November.
I'm always wishing that you're here.
The first couple weeks, I remember,
I thought you'd disappear.

I am weak and you know I'm afraid.
I should have kissed you the morning
after Taking Back Sunday.
You were standing there,
beautiful with your smirk,
against the wall in your white shirt.

Every day
we would dance our own parade,
and play our songs,
'cause there's nowhere we belong.
And never mind the weather—
we can always sleep forever.
I don't know how to say
I love you always.

## CITY ON A HILL

Outside Waterloo
in a corner of a place called Hawkesville,
by firelight a Mennonite family
was wondering what to do.
When a rogue horse leaves you in the snow
and your son's got a broken bone
who could refuse a car ride home?

And so the gritty desperate lawlessness of love
made them question all they thought they
     knew.
By lantern light the Mennonite council told
     that family
to go live somewhere new.

She keeps on telling me the night
was over long before it started.
Nothing stops her now
or makes her move
but some hand of God
sketching out a plan of action
far across the sea.
Where there's a will
there's a city on a hill.

She tied the knot with a railway worker
pipe smoker guitar player,
but over time she saw the signs,
moved out with the kids,
and people called her a heartbreaker.

When a mother outlives her firstborn child
it's hard to crack a smile.
But she knows in heaven
they'll all be reconciled.

She was a teacher who could reach the kids
who no one else believed could make
    something of themselves.
Now she feeds the poor and teaches English
    in the desert
where dreams never leave the wishing well.

She keeps on telling me the night
was over long before it started.
Nothing stops her now
or makes her move
but some hand of God
sketching out a plan of action
far across the sea.
Where there's a will
there's a city on a hill.

# AFTERWORD

*CASPIAN SAWCZAK*

I can recall an interesting conversation I once had, probably about ten years ago, with a family friend who is a professional musician and music teacher: we were talking about the experience of writing music. I was telling him that I thought writing a song often felt much more like discovering—and then revealing to others—something that has already been created by something or someone else. At first I thought that maybe this is only how it *seems* to us rookie writers who don't really know what we're doing and are operating by some haphazard process of verbo-sonic free association. But to my delight, our family friend validated my view of things by affirming that he, too, regularly experienced songwriting in this way. (And I think I later came across a Led Zeppelin interview in which either Plant or Page was saying something similar, about how certain songs almost feel as if they're being dictated to you.) This is probably the sort of thing I had in mind when I made that remark about Bob Dylan's "It Ain't Me Babe" that Luke recounts in the preface.

With this in mind, I'll say that the older I get, the less responsible I feel for much of the music I wrote when I was younger. The vast majority of my catalogue was written either when I was a teenager or during the few short years between high school and university when I was taking art classes and working as a designer. And, at the risk of coming across as a narcissist (or, worse yet, some kind of self-proclaimed prophet-minstrel), I'd say that I agree with Luke's comment about seeing interesting new things in my lyrics when I revisit the old songs from time to time.

I feel like I must have been quite a different person back then. Indeed, the aspiring psychologist in me thinks of the fact that a group of brain structures known collectively as the "limbic system", which are very important for recognizing and responding to emotionally salient stimuli, tend to mature and become more fully functional during adolescence than does the frontal cortex. The latter brain area tends to develop much more during one's twenties. Not only is the frontal cortex responsible for regulating the impulsive inclinations of the limbic system in the service of more adaptive decision-making, the proper functioning of this area seems to bear great significance for the aspects of our behaviour that those close to us recognize as characterizing our unique personalities. Thus, when you consider that my brain was rather different when I wrote the songs contained in this volume, maybe it really is accurate to say that I was a different person back then. If that's the case, how much credit should I take today for the labours of that youth of yesteryear? (Granted, my answer to this question may hinge on whether someone decides they'd like to buy the rights to these songs!)

To get at what's really on my mind, I've found that, especially these days, my friends and family promote my music to a much greater extent than I myself do. And maybe the hesitation on my part stems from the feeling that so much of my music expresses the heart of someone I used to be but no longer am. Thus, I'm not entirely sure how to interact with this material except by occasionally re-listening to it in private and either being pleasantly surprised and impressed by my former self or being embarrassed and amused and having a good laugh; and by sharing a few songs now and then with individuals who for some reason express interest in hearing them. My friends and family have always been tremendously supportive of my musical endeavours, but it's also flattering when I meet someone new and they say they'd like to give my old stuff a listen.

A little while ago, Luke and I arranged to meet on the University of Toronto campus one night and went through my catalogue with coffee, making subtle edits and deciding which songs should be included and how they should be organized. I had a lot of fun working with Luke, but the reason I mention the experience is because I felt like the editorial decisions we made were guided by unspoken intuition just as often as they were by rational discussion. What was so cool about this process was the surprisingly high (though not total) reliability with which Luke's intuitions and mine seemed to be in alignment, which suggested to me, once again, that the final creative product might be something that already existed, independent of either of us; something that we were merely trying to identify and bring to light.

Anyway, I don't know whether you, Dear Reader, have enjoyed these lyrics or would attest to the veracity of the description of them that I've suggested above. But thank you for reading all the same.

*Toronto*
*April 2015*

# ACKNOWLE DGEMENTS

I'm very grateful to my family (not only for their support but also for putting up with so many years of my recording noisy music in my "home studio"), my friends for telling me my music is worthwhile, encouraging me to make more of it, sharing it with others, and coming out to watch me perform, those really nice individuals who were in the position to give me opportunities to share my music, Luke for the project idea, and everyone for listening.

—*Caspian*

To Guy Allen for teaching "Making a Book", in which this collection arose, and for being so flexible as to allow this project; and to everyone I've shared my brother's music with and who shared my enthusiasm.

—*Luke*

# ABOUT THE AUTHORS

Caspian Sawczak has written, recorded, and produced more than three albums' worth of original music. Over the years, he has performed at many events and venues across the Greater Toronto Area, including Youth Day at Nathan Philips' Square, the Downtown Milton Street Festival, the Flavours by the Bay Festival in Pickering, a fundraiser for a local chapter of Food for Life Canada, and various pubs, coffee shops, and schools. Among his favourite artists are Third Eye Blind, Matthew Good Band, Bruce Cockburn, Gaslight Anthem, Sloan, Hey Rosetta!, Sufjan Stevens, Counting Crows, Peter Gabriel, and Radiohead. He is currently working towards a doctorate in neuropsychology at the University of Toronto, but still enjoys occasionally performing at open mic nights and jamming with other musicians.

Luke Sawczak is a recent alumnus of the University of Toronto Mississauga, where he was editor-in-chief of the student paper and sought out creative and intellectual stimulation wherever he could find it. His published works include "Royaume", a short nonfiction story in French that was a finalist in the University of Naples' 2013 Napoli Racconti contest. His interests include musical composition, amateur photography, hobby programming, and nature walks. He lives in Georgetown, Ontario.